Forex

A Quick and Easy Guide for Beginners to Start Trading

Copyright © 2017 by Pete Manlow

All rights reserved.

No part of this eBook may be reproduced or transmitted in any form or by any means, electronic or mechanical, including photocopying, recording or by any information storage and retrieval system, without written permission from the author.

The author has made every effort to ensure the accuracy of the information within this book was correct at time of publication. The author does not assume and hereby disclaims any liability to any party for any loss, damage, or disruption caused by errors or omissions, whether such errors or omissions result from accident, negligence, or any other cause.

Pete Manlow

First Published: January 2017

Table of Contents

Introduction: Why Trade Forex? 4

Chapter 1: Getting to know the Foreign Exchange Market 6

Chapter 2: Forex Terms you should Know 12

Chapter 3: Beginner Strategies to Use 25

Chapter 4: An intro to Forex Indicators 32

Chapter 5: Forex Platforms for Beginners 36

Chapter 6: Tips on Forex Needed by all Beginners 40

Conclusion 51

Introduction: Why Trade Forex?

I want to thank you and congratulate you for buying the book, *"Forex: A Quick and Easy Guide for Beginners to Start Trading"*. Who hasn't dreamed of earning money from home, quitting their boring job, and retiring early? Investment can be one path to doing all those things. But where do you start?

Forex stands for foreign exchange, which always traders try to profit from the changing landscapes of foreign currencies and how their values compare to one another. For people with access to the right information, who have taken the time to learn the right skills, it's possible to earn money from this endeavor. In the world of trading, countless options exist for which avenue to go, so why choose Forex? Here are some of the advantages you'll experience by choosing to go this route.

Benefits to Trading Forex:

- **You don't have to Worry about Commissions:** There are no fees for brokerage, no fees related to the government or exchange, and no fees for clearing. Most retail level brokers in foreign exchange gain their compensation in other ways.

- **It's more Direct than other Routes:** Trading currency allows you direct trading abilities, cutting out the middlemen and letting you go straight to the market to find what you need.

- **Low Costs for Transactions:** The typical costs for transactions in Forex are about 0.1 percent or lower when the market is in normal conditions. Comparatively, this is very affordable. Unlike other types of investing and trading, Forex doesn't require that you are already wealthy to get started and begin earning.

- **The Market is Alive 24 Hours a Day:** Another benefit to choosing to trade on the foreign exchange market is the fact that it's alive at all hours. No matter what time it is, the market is open somewhere in the world, making this avenue quite flexible and fit for many different schedules. Some people are most productive when they first wake up in the morning, while others are night owls. You can put in the necessary study hours to learn Forex and then start trading full or part time at whatever times of day you want.

As you can see, there are many reasons why trading foreign exchange is preferable to going with other types of trading. In this book, you will learn all about how to get started with this and begin earning money and enjoying financial freedom. It's important to note that as with any other skill or worthwhile pursuit, there is a learning curve, and this will require patience and dedication. If you follow the guidelines in this book, there's no reason why you can't become a successful Forex trader.

Thanks again for buying this book, I hope you enjoy it!

Chapter 1: Getting to know the Foreign Exchange Market

Although Forex stands for the terms "foreign exchange", what this actually deals with is different currencies. Trading on the Forex market involves changing out one type of currency (such as the US dollar for example) for another type of currency. This decision is made based on a few different factors, typically for commerce or tourism. Since companies and businesses exist over the globe, this requires the need for making transactions with other nations using their country's currency. The value of each currency varies, causing the need for services providing foreign exchange. This much needed and useful service is provided by investment and commercial banks, for the clients they serve, but has also opened up a new opportunity for people to trade currencies against each other online.

Uses for Forex:

- **For Hedge Purposes:** Enterprises on a commercial level, that conduct business in foreign nations are undergoing some measure of risk when they purchase services or goods, or sell services or goods, to other nations. This is because of the fluctuations that naturally occur, over time, in the value of currencies. Essentially, the market of foreign exchange gives an avenue for hedging this risk by giving a solid, fixed rate that the transaction must end at. In order for this to happen, the trader has to sell or buy currency in the swap or forward markets. At this time, the bank decides upon and locks in a decided upon rate, allowing the trader to know what they can expect as an exchange rate, taking proper steps to mitigate risk for the company.

In some ways, the "futures" market can give an avenue for hedging a risk related to currency, depending on the particular currency and trade size. This same market is used in an exchange that has been centralized, and therefore is not as liquid as other markets. This is because those markets have been decentralized and function in the banking system across the globe.

- **For Speculation:** There is always fluctuation happening within the values of nations' currencies, since demand and supply is always changing, along with related factors. Some of those factors are geo-political risks, the strength of the country's economy, tourism, the flow of trade at the time, interest rates, and more. This provides traders the chance to bet along with these fluctuating values, by either selling or buying a currency against another currency, hoping that your purchased currency will rise in value, or that the type of currency you're selling will decrease in comparison with the currency's counterpart.

- **Using Currency for Asset Purposes:** Currency can also be used in this category, which has two specific features. These involve either earning what exists as the difference in interest rate between the two currency types, or gaining some value from the rate of exchange of those currencies.

Why is Trading Currencies Possible?

Until the internet became so widely available, trading currency was only really available to interbank systems, for the purpose of servicing clients. Eventually, banks began setting up a system that allowed them to trade using their personal accounts. This then led to individuals with high net worth, hedge funds, and big multi-national companies. Due to the prevalence of the web, a market based around retail, aimed at traders on an individual level, has started. This market gives simple access to the markets of Forex, by using brokers in a secondary market, or directly through the banks.

Risk in Forex Trading:

There is plenty of confusion out there about currency trading risks. A lot has been mentioned about the unrelated status of the interbank market, which is not regulated and for that reason, quite risky. This judgment is not completely true, however. A more sensible way to approach the subject of Forex risk would be understanding what the distinctions are between a centralized and decentralized market, and figuring out from there where regulation is needed.

- **Regulations for Protection:** Various banks trade amongst themselves throughout the world, which make up an interbank market. These banks must figure out and accept credit and sovereign risk, requiring internal auditing, which helps them stay safe. Regulations are then imposed to protect the banks that are involved.

- **Demand and Supply:** Given the fact that the market is composed of these individual banks giving out bids and offers for a specified currency, the pricing of the market is reached through demand and supply. Given the large flows going on inside of this system, it's very difficult for any specific standalone trader to have much influence on a currency's price in the market. Trillions of dollars are being traded each day, meaning that even the most powerful and influential banks are not able to control the market for long without cooperation or coordination from other powerful banks.

- **The Network of Electronic Communication:** There are current attempts happening to create a network of electronic communication, which would bring sellers and buyers into an exchange that is more centralized, allowing for transparent pricing. This would be a positive development for traders that trade on a retail level, since they will be allowed more competitive prices and liquidity. Banks would, of course, not have the same concerns and could stay decentralized. Traders who have immediate access to banks in the foreign exchange market are not as exposed and vulnerable as traders who trade on a retail level among unregulated and small brokers. Talk about regulation has now come up due to a need for protecting retail traders.

Here is what to Consider getting Started in Forex:

If you hope to start trading in the foreign exchange market, and think about the previous information about broker risk, it's important to consider all pros and cons of doing so. Here are some points to consider and keep in mind:

- **Market Size:** The size of the foreign exchange market is the biggest when it comes to how much is traded throughout the globe, meaning that it also has the highest amount of liquidity. This makes it relatively simple to exit or enter a trading position involving popular currencies in a very short amount of time.

- **Leverage in Forex:** Due to this liquidity, and simplicity of exiting or entering trades, brokers and banks can offer big amounts of leverage, meaning that traders have control over big positions, using a smaller amount of money than is needed with other types of trading. Traders have to understand how to use leverage, along with the risks that come along with it. In order for leverage to be beneficial, however, it must be used cautiously and judiciously. Not understanding this can lead to devastating consequences in the account of the trader.

- **Availability and Flexibility:** This was mentioned briefly in the intro, but the Forex markets work 24 hours a day, beginning in the country of Australia and closing down in the city of New York. The main Forex centers of trading are New York, London, Paris, Frankfurt, Hong Kong, Sydney, Singapore, and Tokyo.

- **The Big Picture:** Another benefit to trading currency is that it focuses on the overall, larger picture of various nations and their economies, along with the way they connect with and influence each other. Only then can they understand what it is that affects the values of currency. Some find it simpler and easier to look at the activity happening on an economic level, in order to help them decide which trading decisions to make. Unlike other types of trading, knowing about knowledge specific to particular industries, opportunities in the market, and financial and management skills of companies are not necessary to succeed with foreign exchange trading.

How should you Approach the Foreign Exchange Market?

For the majority of traders or investors who have experience with the stock market, there must be a change in perspective in order to successfully switch to Forex, or to add it to their repertoire as an extra income avenue. Trading currency has been described as the opportunity of active traders. This makes it suitable for brokers who will earn more when traders are offering high activity. Forex trading is also described as leveraged, meaning that it's simpler for traders to begin without a large amount of cash, which may not be necessary when it comes to trading the stock market.

In addition to trading to earn profits, Forex can be a useful way to hedge your portfolio. If you, for instance, build up your portfolio somewhere that allows potential for a stock's value to increase, but there are some downsides, in terms of risk, with currency. Every type of trading comes with different risks, so you should make your choice according to what's important to you and your investment needs.

Chapter 2: Forex Terms you should Know

There is no reason why you have to limit yourself to only one type of investing, but it's good to start with one specific type when you are first starting out. You are probably very excited to begin learning about Forex and get started as soon as possible so you can earn money. This chapter will help you become familiar with the most used terms in Forex. It's not important to memorize every word before you have a full understanding of each of them. This section will be a reference that you can check any time you are uncertain in the future. This is only meant to serve as a first step to getting familiar with some of the foreign exchange jargon typically used.

Understanding Currency Pairs:

One of the first things you'll probably take note of when getting familiar with trading foreign exchange is the mention of currency pairs. When you imagine the price of specific objects, it's simple to grasp, since only one price exists. When trading something like oil, for example, a price is given for each barrel. When gold is traded, prices are quoted per ounce.

- **One Single Price:** In foreign exchange, there is typically a single price mentioned also, but it's in regards to a pair of currencies, or what is known as a currency pair. To beginners, this may be confusing, so this section will explain how that works. When currencies are being traded, you are selling and buying that currency as it relates to another one. You don't just buy euros for example; you buy them using a specific amount of a different type of currency. This means that if you have U.S. dollars, and need to trade them for euros, you're using a specific amount of the dollars to do this. That currency pair would be called EUR/USD.

- **Denoting Currency Pairs:** There are specified ways that currency pairs are denoted, and these must be learned before you proceed. When the currency pair in question is the U.S. dollar and the euro, it's stated as EUR/USD, and not the other way around.

Exchange Rates:

For example, let's say that a EUR/USD currency pair costs $1.40. To put it another way, for each euro you are purchasing, you are paying $1.40. The price of this currency pair is the rate of exchange for the number of units the second currency needed to purchase one unit of the first one. So, a rate of exchange of 1.4 for the currency pair of EUR/USD translates to the fact that you need 1.4 U.S. dollars to purchase a single euro. If, in the future, the U.S. dollar appreciates in value or becomes stronger, you don't need as many U.S. dollars to purchase more euros. But, since the dollar has gotten stronger, which is shown in relation to another currency (the euro), or the second type of currency in the pair, the overall price decreases in the EUR/USD pair.

If the currency pair EUR/USD goes down in value to $1.30, or 1,3, the dollar has gone up in value in relation to the euro. In other words, the euro has gotten weaker while the dollar has gotten stronger. If, therefore, the EUR/USD price decreases to 1.3, for each euro you wish to purchase, you'll only have to spend 1.3 dollars. You don't actually need to have dollars on hand to purchase this currency pair. In fact, you can begin with Great British pounds to make this purchase. You would be converting your GBP into dollars, and then using those dollars to purchase euros. Even though trading Forex means that things are automatically done for you, it's useful to be aware of what's happening behind this trade.

Base and Quote Currencies in the Currency Pair:

The original currency in a pair of currencies is known as the base, which has an inherent value of one. The second one is called a quote currency, which refers to how much you need to pay to get one single unit of the base.

Pips for tracking Movements of Currency:

When studying and learning the ropes of Forex, you will notice that pips are mentioned quite a lot. A pip refers to the measurement of the distance a price has shifted or moved. In fact, pip is a shortened version of "percentage in point." When you decide to consider the rate of exchange between the dollar and pound (which would be denoted as GBP/USD), you may consider it as, for example, 1.52, with only two numbers after the point. But in the market of foreign exchange, this gets broken down and we see a price such as 1.5200.

The very last number in that sequence of numbers is known as the pip. When a currency pair's value shifts from 1.5200 to 1.5201, it is said that the value has moved by just one pip. Pips allow traders to measure what they are earning in profits. When a trader purchases a pair of currencies, still using the GPB/USD at 1.5200 for example, and the price increases to 1.5240, the trade is said to have gained a profit of 40 pips. Some brokers even break these prices down further by including something called a "pipette", or a fifth number. This will explain why, sometimes, you see five figures instead of four after a decimal point when you're checking out prices for currency pairs.

Knowing your Currency Spreads:

The simplest method for understanding "spreads" in Forex is by considering them as your broker fees. If a pair of currencies is at a set price, for example 1.3 for the EUR/USD pair of currencies, you will not be buying them at that price. Instead, the broker will give you a price that is slightly higher than that, of 1.3001 or 1.3002 for example. When you're trying to sell, they won't buy the pair at the original 1.3000, but would instead go for 1.2999 or something similar.

Buy, Sell, and the Bid Ask Price:

Obviously, there is a distinction between 1.3001 and 1.2999, which would be described as two pips. The spread is that difference. In other words, a spread is the value difference between what price your broker is buying from you or selling to you. In order to earn profit, the broker must be from you at a slightly lower price and sell it higher.

- **The Bid in Forex Trading:** A bid refers to the best price that a trader can purchase what is being traded at the present moment. In the market of foreign exchange, the price known as the bid is the limit price at which a broker will purchase that instrument from you.

- **The Ask in Forex Trading:** An "ask" in Forex refers to the best price that a trader is able to sell what is being traded at the present moment. In the market of foreign exchange, an ask price refers to the lowest or best price a broker is willing to sell you the instrument.

Foreign Exchange Charts:

Charts will show you the action of a price as it moves over time. In other words, a chart gives you a representation, on a visual level, of the action of a price, allowing you to use this information in your analyses. It allows you to keep an eye on the rate of exchange, or price, of a pair of currency as it shifts through time. When it comes to looking at price charts, a currency pair's price will be listed on the right on a vertical axis (the rate of exchange for the number of units required to purchase one of the base or first currency.) At the bottom, along the horizontal axis, is the timeline for this. Here are some terms related to charts that you should take note of:

- **Japanese Candlestick:** This is a method for showing the movement of a price. This can give you a specific amount of useful data and information, including whether or not the price has moved up. This information is shown by color, which is set ahead of time by the individual trader according to their preference. These colors will automatically change as the candle forms a bullish or bearish.

- **What Candlesticks Show**: Candlesticks show the open, close, low, and high, covering any time period from a month to just one minute. On a chart that shows a minute, the candlesticks require a single minute to take shape. After a minute has passed, the candle finishes forming as a new one starts. On charts that are hourly, the candle will require one hour to form, so on and so forth. Candlesticks can also show you the opening and closing prices for the periods they represent. If, for example, you're looking at a candlestick of four hours, it will give you information about the opening prices at the beginning of that period, along with its closing price. In addition, candlesticks show the lowest and highest price during the time period that the candle was forming.

Foreign Exchange Trading Platforms:

Another useful concept to know about is trading platforms for Forex. A platform like this is the place where your orders are put in to either purchase or sell, or both, in some cases. Essentially, this platform is a center of command that allows you to open up trades. In addition to that, you use it to tell your broker the following:

- What you wish to sell or buy.
- How much will be bought or sold.
- When your profit will be taken if you succeed.
- When to close or accept a loss if you don't succeed.

Nearly all platforms for trading give the option of similar functions and charts for pricing. There is no shortage of trading platforms to choose from, so do your research and find the one that suits your needs the best. In chapter five, we will give you some platforms to check out and start with.

Assets and Financial or Trading Instruments:

These terms are all used to describe what is currently being traded. If oil is being traded, for example, that is the current instrument being referred to. If a currency pair, such as EUR/USD is being traded, that is the instrument in question. This is also described as an asset, in some cases.

Closing or Opening Positions:

When you have either short sold or bought an instrument, it is said that you just opened up a trading position. This means that selling and buying is, at times, referred to as entering into a trading position. This is also known as entering into the market. Once you, as a trader, exit out of the market, you are said to be closing your position.

- **Entering:** You are making an entry, as a trader, when you make the decision to open your position, by either selling or buying an instrument.

- **Exiting:** An exit refers to the instance when the trader closes out their current, open position, taking either a loss or a profit.

Stop Losses in Foreign Exchange Trading:

Stop losses essentially allow your account some protection. If your trade begins going in an unfavorable direction, it will prevent you from losing everything, or losing more than you need to. For example, if you just purchased an asset and you begin to lose money because the trade is going south, your entire account is under threat depending on whether that price continues going the wrong way for you. Your stop loss would place an order that would close this trade immediately, once it reaches the point you have decided is not acceptable.

What are Profit Targets?

Profit targets are the prices that you choose to exit the market at, taking what you have earned in profit. Generally, these are decided beforehand as the trader decides to enter into the market, meaning that before you get into the market, you are aware of how much profit to expect, if all goes how you hope it will. Successful traders know how to leave when this happens, instead of sticking around, hoping that they will earn more, and risking losing. This is one of the many reasons that emotional control matters in foreign exchange trading.

The Bear and Bull Concepts in Forex Trading:

- **A Bear:** This refers to the type of trader who believes a market will go down or fall. When a trader has this idea, they are known as being bearish, or simply, a "bear". An easy way to remember this concept is by imagining the way bears fight, by using their paws in a downward swiping motion.

- **A Bull:** This refers to the type of trader who thinks that the market is going to go up, or rise. When a trader believes that, they are described as bullish or simply, a "bull". An easy way to remember this concept is by imagining a bull fighting and using their horns by swiping them upward.

Long Forex Trading Positions:

When something is referred to, in Forex, as "long", it's considered to be going upward. You have a "long" position once you just opened up your trade and also purchased something. You might hear investors and traders saying things like "I am long right now" or that they went long at a certain price. What this means is that they have entered into a position of buying. When it comes to foreign exchange trading, when traders think that a pair of currency will rise, leading them to buy it, that would be called entering a position that is long.

Short Selling Trading Positions:

The idea of "long" when it comes to trading is not that hard to understand. You just hit the "buy" option, which enters you into the long position. That price then either rises or falls. When it increases, you earn, when it decreases, you are losing money. If you believe a price will decrease and you have yet to enter into the market, you have an option of hitting the "sell" option and going into a short sell. This essentially means that you've sold an item that is not yours, in order to purchase it back, with a differing cost. To put it simply, when you short sell something and then the price decreases, you are earning, and if it goes up, you're losing.

The Ratio of Risk to Reward in Forex Trading:

When the ratio of risk to reward is referred to, it's about the ratio of what you're risking on a particular trade, with what you are making in the most ideal scenario. This means that if you're risking $15, that's how much you are willing to possibly lose. If your trade fails or doesn't go in your favor, you're aware of what you're risking and won't lose more than what you put in. If your hope is to gain $45, that is your ideal reward, which you should have believed can happen based on knowledge and analysis. This would mean that your ratio is 1 to 3, since you're risking $15 in hopes of gaining $45.

Put and Call Options in Foreign Exchange:

Before going into the definitions for put and call options, it's important to first refer to currency options. The subject of currency options starts when a seller and buyer start up a contract that gives the buyer the right to either sell or buy a certain amount of currency, at a specific price, either before or on the date of expiration. But the buyer might or might not sell or purchase it. What is involved in currency options?

- The first element involved in a currency option is the amount or premium that a buyer is paying a seller.
- Next, there is the strike price, which is also called the exercise price or the price that has been predetermined. Every currency has an existing value in the market which is known as a spot price.
- Lastly, there's the date of expiration of a contract to consider. When a buyer doesn't choose to exercise their option by the time this date passes, they are losing a premium.

Defining the Terms:

Now that you have a basic understanding of currency options and what they mean, we can move on to put and call options, which are two types.

- **A Call Option:** A call option is the right of a buyer to purchase a currency at its strike price. In the standpoint of a buyer, he is hoping and expecting that the strike price will go up, while a seller will be expecting and hoping for the opposite. As soon as a buyer can purchase the currency at a higher rate than its market value or spot price, they can exercise their call option. An example of this would be a security being traded at $50. You could then hope or anticipate that it would rise to $60. This could lead you to purchase a call option at $55 at a price of 20 cents.

    If you saw that the security went up to $60, you could still purchase it for $55, regardless of its $60 value. You would then be earning almost $5 in profit for each share. In addition, whoever sold you that call would have to also sell you its security at a price of $55, and at an almost $5 loss. If you see that the security doesn't go over $55 by the date of expiration, this call will expire, becoming completely worthless, leading the one who purchased the call to have lost 20 cents, while the seller keeps that same amount.

- **A Put Option:** Next we have a put option. This lets a buy sell off a currency at its set strike price. The buyer will then hope that the value will go down, as the seller hopes that it will go up. Then it's the buyer who will exercise their put option at a time when that currency's spot price is lower than its strike price. For example, say a security is being traded for a rate of $50, and you think that it's going to decrease to just $40. Then, you would purchase a "put" selection, spending 20 cents of your money. If you saw that the security went down to what you projected, you would be able to sell it at a rate of $45, regardless of its $40 value.

You would then earn almost $5 per share here. On the same side of things, whoever sold you that option would have to purchase the $45 security and take on the loss of nearly $5. If it turned out that the security didn't go under $45 by its date of expiration, it would expire completely worthless, leading the purchaser of the put option to lose their 20 cents, while the seller keeps it.

As soon as a trader has set up a call option for a currency, they can buy a specified amount of said currency at a specific value price. For instance, a "call" choice might allow them to buy 300 Japanese Yen for 200 U.S. dollars up until the date of expiration for this option. Also, the put option allows the person holding it to sell off a certain amount of that currency at a specified value price.

What are Currency Gains in Forex?

This section will cover some basic tricks to remember to heighten your chance of gains when it comes to trades in currency options.

- **Money Options:** When it comes to these, try to buy at or in them whenever you can. The bigger the difference when it comes to the spot and strike prices, the less likely the instance that gains will occur on that particular trade avenue.

- **Mind the Date of Expiration:** Always pay attention to the date of expiration. When the date is further away, that is always preferred to one with a closer expiration date. When the end date of an option is closer, the time will elapse faster, while an option premium is going to decay in all likelihood, as the expiration nears. In other words, try to work with, rather than against time, while trading.

The above should have given you a clear picture of put and call options. Now that you have that understanding, you will know how to trade in the market of currency and stocks. But make sure that before you exercise any options at all, you're done the research necessary and aren't going to go overboard. Think about options that have at least a month or two before they expire for the best results, especially when you are just starting out and learning the ropes.

Margin in the Foreign Exchange Market:

For beginner traders, margin can sound like a new and confusing concept and it's also easy to misunderstand. Essentially, margin is a deposit you make in good faith that holds a position open and offers collateral. Usually, margin is confused with an extra fee to those trading. In reality, this is not a cost for transaction, but simply an amount from the equity in your account allocated and set aside as a deposit for margin. When you trade using margin, you should keep in mind that the value needed for holding a position open is dependent upon the size of the trade. As that goes up, so will the requirement for the margin.

Leverage in the Foreign Exchange Market:

Leverage can be called margin's byproduct. It allows a trader to have control over trades that are larger in size. Most traders utilize this in order to maximize what they earn in their returns. This is important to get across; losses also get maximized when you are using leverage. This means that it's crucial to keep in mind that you should control leverage if you use it.

Chapter 3: Beginner Strategies to Use

The market of foreign exchange is very liquid and involves a large number of traders and investors. In addition to this, it's been very well established. As is logical this means that the time and popularity that has gone into this market has led to traders everywhere coming up with strategy after strategy for success. As a beginner, the amount of techniques and information out there on this subject can be intimidating, to say the least. Certain strategies are confusing, daunting, and have a steep and tough learning curve. When you're just starting out, the last thing you want to do is confuse yourself.

The Simpler, the Better, at First:

For newcomers to this market, it's always better to begin using a strategy that is simple. Think of it as the simpler your technique is, the better your chance of understanding it (and therefore succeeding with it) is. You have no shortage of time to get more complicated with it once you have learned all of the basics of Forex. Whether or not you come up with a complex or simple technique, keep in mind that your philosophy should be to only utilize what will work for you. For people who are very new to trading, it's uncommon to have a lot of free time to dedicate to staying on top of trade developments. For them, it's always better to stick with simple techniques, which will allow for a low maintenance and effective approach to trading.

Strategies for Forex Beginners:

This chapter will give you a few foolproof beginner strategies to use. The first couple of strategies are going to rely on following market trends, while the third one tries to show you how to earn profits from differentials in interest rates, instead of relying on the directions of the market. To start with, we first have to define what a trend is. A trend is a pattern that you have observed that the market is moving in, and the tendency for that to continue.

Following Trends in the Market:

This system tries to produce sell and buy signals that will correspond with new trends forming. Many different methods exist for identifying where the trend begins and ends, and a lot of the strategies that are simple for Forex follow similar techniques and methods.

- **They are tough to Stick with:** Following trends can often lead to big profits, and many traders can boast amazing track records from using this strategy. However, strategies that rely on this do come with their drawbacks, such as the fact that they can be hard to stay with, and that big trends don't happen as often as other developments in the market.

- **Plenty of Losing Trades:** In addition to this, conditions that show that a trend might be starting don't happen often. In other words, this strategy does tend to come with plenty of trades that lose. The idea behind going with these types of strategies is that any losses will be made up for in large, but less frequent, successful and profitable trades. This sounds simple on the surface, but it's harder than it sounds to follow in practice. In addition to this, you usually end up giving back a large amount of your earnings. When trends fail, this isn't very easy to withstand as a trader.

- **Deep Pockets help with this:** In order to properly utilize this system, you should ideally have a lot of capital to spare. When you don't have to worry about the capital you're using, your chances of losing in an extended downward trend are minimized.

So following trends can be helpful for beginners, but less ideal for those who are not wealthy. Now it's time to get down to some strategies for trading. Our first technique relies on identifying the time that a trend is starting to form by looking to indicators known as price breakouts.

Price Breakouts:

Markets, at times, oscillate between resistance and support, which is also called consolidation. When the market goes past its consolidation boundaries and reaches new lows or highs, this is called a breakout. If a new trend is to happen, a breakout has to first happen. Therefore, they are seen as possible signs that a new trend is starting or is about to start. The hard aspect to this is that not every breakout will lead to a new trend.

Why you should Consider Managing Risk:

When it comes to Forex, or any type of trading and investment for that matter, even simple strategies need to think about managing risk. When you do this, you minimize what you might lose as the trend breaks down.

- **Highs and Lows:** If you notice that a new high is happening, this could mean the beginning of a trend going upward. On the other hand, seeing that a new low has been reached shows that the beginning of a downward trend might be happening.

- **Reacting Fast**: When you react fast to these trends, you can ride it out early on, but you might end up following trends that exist within a shorter period of time.

A Breakout Strategy for Long Term:

The signal to buy is when you see a price break out over the high of 20 days. The signal to sell is when you see a price break out under the low of 20 days. This is easy and simple, but a huge drawback exists regardless. Mainly that new highs don't necessarily turn out to be a new trend moving upward, and that new lows being reached don't always lead to a downward trend. This means that false signals are plentiful when relying on this technique, as mentioned before.

- **Exiting the Trade:** You can alleviate this issue by using a stop loss, or by knowing how to properly exit trades when they aren't going in your favor. One good way to do this is using an approach based on time. This involves just closing out your position once a specific amount of time has gone by. This allows you to get out before things get sticky and stick with that principle no matter what. For example, you can decide to enter into a trade and then exit it after 80 days elapses.

- **Using a Shorter Method:** The strategy above is for longer term trades, but if you discover that you aren't receiving signals frequently enough, you can adjust them accordingly. You could, for example, start using hours, rather than days, to employ a strategy in the short term.

A Crossover Strategy for Moving Averages:

This strategy uses the principle of moving averages, which uses old data about prices and doesn't move as quickly as the present price of the market. The more time that exists in this average, the slower it will go. Oftentimes, you will use a longer average along with a shorter one. Let's take an average of 25 days for the shorter one, and an average of 200 days for the other. When you look at a chart showing these, the faster and shorter moving average shows a trend change when it crosses over the long one. On the other hand, when you see the short moving average going above the long one, the new prices are surpassing old ones.

- **The Signal to Buy:** The above information shows that there is a bullish movement happening in the trend and signals that you should buy. On the other hand, when your short moving average goes under the longer one, it shows that there may be a bearish movement and that you should sell. Instead of only being utilized to make signals of trading, these moving averages can be used to confirm that there is, in fact, a trend occurring overall.

- **Combining the Two:** You can then confirm these two methods using your moving averages for confirmation, in order to heighten the effectiveness of your breakout signals. Using this strategy, you get rid of signals that aren't aligned with the trends seen overall and shown by the moving averages. If you receive a signal to buy from the existing breakout, you should look to check if your short moving average is going above the longer one. When you see that it is, that's when you place your trade. If it isn't, you wait.

The Carry Trade Strategy for Beginners:

This last strategy is important to know for beginners, and is also used by successful and professional traders. Most importantly, it's simple and easy to understand and put into use. The foundation of this strategy is to earn profit using the yield difference that exists between two different currencies. In order to get an understanding of what else is involved here, let's think about a person who converts currency physically. Envision a person borrowing an amount of Japanese currency; the yen. Since the interest rate on Japanese currency is usually pretty late, what it will cost to hold this is not significant at all.

Interest making up for Debt Financing:

Then the theoretical trader exchanges this money into CAD (Canadian dollars), investing the earnings into a bond, yielding .6 percent. This interest being received should ideally exceed what it costs to finance the debt from the Japanese currency. However, there are always possible drawbacks to consider; in this case, a risk is involved with this trade. If the Japanese currency grew in value enough up against the CAD, this would lead to the trader losing some of their investment. These principles also apply to trading Forex, but the convenient aspect is that it all occurs in one place (the trade).

The Risks Involved in this Strategy:

If you purchased a pair of currency where the base currency has a high rate of interest up against the quote currency, your trading account would benefit from this positive rate of exchange. The amount earned from this correlates with the amount commanded of currency, meaning that leverage is helpful when the strategy does work. As mentioned before, there's always a risk involved in this that you would lose from the movement throughout the pair.

- **Choosing the Correct Currencies:** In this strategy, you should look for a Forex currency pair that is low in volatility. Remember that leverage adds to your losses when you're on the losing end of this. Yen is popular for this method, as a funding currency. This is because the rates of Japanese currency have basically always been low and the money is viewed as very stable and reliable. The use of this strategy helps to support it since the more traders who use it, the higher the pressure to sell off the currency used to fund it.

- **Considering Low Interest:** Keep in mind that due to the environment of low interest, the differentials between interest rates will also be affected. Keep this in mind if you opt for this strategy, and always only trade with what you can afford to lose, of course.

Keep in mind that this is not a scheme to get rich quick, and that it requires plenty of practice and a serious state of mind to see any success with it. This is something that anyone who is willing to learn, can learn and begin earning from, but only if they are committed to it. When you're first starting out with learning about this, try to see it as you would any other job. You have to put hours of your day into it to see any results from the time you're giving to it. Once you start to get the hang of the market and earn profits, all of the time you put it will be more than worth it, especially since this can be your path to financial freedom and early retirement.

Chapter 4: An intro to Forex Indicators

Quantitative, technical, fundamental; these are all methods that traders in Forex use to try to predict currency pair movements. Does this sound intimidating to you? Well, keep in mind that all successful and professional traders started out as beginners who didn't know what those words meant. As they learned the ropes of the foreign exchange market, they developed the necessary skills to master it. Now, the most successful traders have varying methods. Some of them will read news, focus on interest rates, and look to variables in economics to decide how to make their trading decisions, while other traders would rather use indicators and chart tools to help inform their decisions for trading.

Basics in Forex Indicators:

Regardless of the method you choose to trade, you have to figure out how to view and interpret a Forex chart. Thankfully, this chapter will serve you as a great starting point. First, you have to understand the basics that are involved before moving on to more advanced methods. As mentioned earlier in the book Forex refers to foreign exchange, and consists of purchasing and selling off various types of currency in the market in hopes of earning money from it. In the market of Forex, institutions, speculators, investors, and retailers determine the value that will appear between currencies.

- **Reading Charts:** A chart, in Forex, is a graphical image of the rate of exchange happening between a couple of currencies. This shows the way a rate of exchange has occurred and shifted as time has gone by. It would, for example, show the changes in the relationship between the U.S. dollar and the Euro over time.

- **Timeframes in Charts:** Another important consideration when learning about this is the way timeframes work in charts. The time period that a chart will show will depend on what you select for it to show. Many Forex charts are set, at default, to 24 hour timeframes, but others exist over longer or shorter periods of time. Each displayed point on this chart, either a bar, a candle, or a line, will show the data for trading within that day (or whatever time period it is showing). If you shifted the timeframe from 24 hours to one hour, every point in that chart would be showing an hour of data regarding trading.

The majority of free tools for charting Forex developments give you options between timeframes, from 60 seconds to 30 days. With the software that is even more advanced for charting Forex developments, more choices are available.

Different Chart Types in Forex:

Traders in Forex have come up with a few different types of charts to decipher and interpret data related to their trades. The main types of charts are candlesticks (which we briefly talked about in chapter two), bar charts, and line charts. For most traders in Forex, the candlestick options appear to be most popular, and it's simple to understand why that is once you understand it more.

- **Why are Candlesticks so Popular?** In comparison with the line chart option, which displays prices from the price close to the next close, the charts with candlesticks show more than three times the amount of data, showing not only the close, but the high and low price, and open of a certain period of time. When you have access to this data, you are able to study the way prices have moved throughout various time periods, rather than only when they were closed.

- **The Colored Portions:** The green and read parts of the candle on the chart are called the body, which represents the difference of the closing and opening price of the relevant currency of the chart, throughout a specified period of time. If the candle has an opening price worth less than the price at closing, the color of the candle's body is green. If, on the other hand, it goes opposite than this, meaning that its opening price ends up being higher than its price at closing, this will lead to a red candle color.

- **Shadows or Wicks:** On the candlestick charts you can see black lines both below and above the candles themselves, which are named shadows or wicks. These represent the lowest and highest prices that were reached within the specific period of time that the chart is representing.

The bars on a candlestick show the low to high range using a straight, vertical line. But when it comes to charting with candlesticks, the body or larger block in the center of the chart shows the existing range between closing and opening prices during the time period. If this block at the center is colored or filled in, it typically means that the pair of currency closed out lower than the price that it opened at. When the price at closing is higher than it was at opening, the center block is unfilled, hollow, or simply white.

Line Charts in the Foreign Exchange Market:

Line charts in Forex, made simply, draw a single line, starting at one price of closing, to another. When these are strung in succession using a line, it's possible to see the general movement of the price of a pair of currency as it shifts over a specific time period. This can help people with trying to predict how the prices will move in the future.

Bar Charts in the Foreign Exchange Market:

Bar charts are a bit more complicated than line charts. They will show closing and opening prices of currency pairs, along with the lows and the highs of those currency pairs.

- **Lowest Prices:** During the specified period of time, the lowest price of trading is indicated by the bottom section of a vertical bar, hence the name bar charts. On the top section of that bar, the highest paid price can be seen.

- **The Overall Range:** The actual bar shows the trading range of the currency pair altogether, as one whole. To the left of this bar there is a horizontal hash which represents the price at opening, with the hash on the right-hand side shows the price at closing.

When you see the word bar used in Forex information, make sure you are aware of the period of time it is meant to be referring to. A bar is just a specified period of time, which could be an hour, week, or day. Another name for bar charts is OHLC charts. Using currency charts as a beginner is a great way to evaluate the behaviors of the market, to figure out which direction the currencies will head next. In order to make sense of what you read on the chart as far as currency movements, traders have come up with indicators, which are essentially differing visual guides (such as the moving averages discussed in the previous chapter.)

Chapter 5: Forex Platforms for Beginners

With countless brokers in the foreign exchange world for a beginner to pick from, it can be confusing and overwhelming to begin. Newcomers to Forex should try to choose a platform for trading that is safe and well-established, in addition to being simple to use, and easy. While it's true that spreads and fees are important considerations to think about, they should come second to opting for a broker that's easy to use and reputable.

Recommended Platforms to Start with:

There are not exactly brokers in Forex that are specifically designed for newcomers and beginners, but some brokers offer free education programs and practice (demo) accounts that can help you learn the basics. Here are some brokers that will offer this to you, as a Forex beginner.

- **ETX Capital to begin with:** If you are hoping to find a Forex platform that is professional, ETX Capital is a good choice. This is a reputable broker that is officially regulated by a financial overseer company in the United Kingdom. This resource has been operating for more than a decade, meaning that they are very established and offer quality client support for those who need it. In addition to this, ETX is simple and easy to operate, but is less social or modern than other platforms. If you are hoping to find a platform that is more like what the professions would use, this is a good choice. In addition, they allow you to join for free with a demo account, letting you practice. Check out their site to learn more.

- **Markets.com for Foreign Exchange Beginners:** You could probably tell by the name of this platform, but this resource offers information and tools for those of you learning how to operate within the complex market of foreign exchange. Stocks, indices, and commodities are able to be accessed and a high number of different pairs of currency to choose from are available. Yet another great quality of this platform is the frequency with which their information gets updated, keeping it relevant. This information includes professional commentary from experienced traders, how to data and videos, current news, and analyses of the market.

  Instead of having to scour the internet of read through multiple websites each day, this allows for traders to get all of their information in one spot and stay on top of their trades. Support for customers is offered in many languages and at all times of the day.

- **eToro to get Started with:** This is a good choice for people who are newly entering the market of Forex. Their design and concept draws in traders at every level of skill, and they offer a few different systems for varying needs of their clients. But one quality that stands out about this platform is their open book system, which is similar to a social media platform within the website. Newcomers to the foreign exchange world can follow successful trading professionals as they work in real time. This allows for the understanding of when specific trades must be employed, and what to avoid, as well.

  This offers a great opportunity for beginners to gain knowledge second-hand which isn't offered by many other brokers. The services of customer support on this platform are also quite impressive, completely with e-mail, phone numbers, and live support over chat. They offer support in almost 20 different languages and a multilingual support staff.

- **AVA Trade for your Beginner Trades:** This platform started in '06 and is believed to be among the biggest of all Forex online brokers on the planet. You can choose from stocks, CFDs, or of course, foreign exchange, to trade with. This site is regulated by Ireland's central bank, among other bodies of government, making it safe and trustworthy. Another defining feature of this platform is that it offers a variety of platforms to trade on, letting beginners decide which is most suitable for their needs. These are all available to traders regardless of the size of the account they will be using.

  The center of education on this site provides tools like economic calendars, updates on the market (live), webinars, trading guides, and video tutorial guides. In a lot of respects, this area lets beginners get a deep look at the market before they decide to take a specific position. They offer email, telephone, and chat as customer support in multiple languages, and at all hours of the day and night.

- **XM.com as a Trading Platform:** One major advantage to this site is that it only requires a five dollar deposit to start trading (which should only be done after you have done plenty of practice on a demo account, of course.) This system is accurate and user-friendly, even for beginners. If you want to test this out before you decide to risk your real capital, you have $100,000 of fake money to play around with in a demo account. Transparency and security are not issues on this site since it's regulated by financial authorities in Cyprus.

The above are just a few of what successful and professional traders think of as the best brokers in Forex online for beginners. All of these resources give the insight and clarity needed to make great choices at the right times. Establishing good habits at the beginning of your trading career is crucial, since these habits will carry on as you advance in your knowledge and expertise. With the advent of social media on these platforms as well as quality materials for educating beginners, anyone can now benefit from the services they offer and begin earning with Forex. These days, becoming a profitable trader in the foreign exchange market is easier than it's ever been.

Chapter 6: Tips on Forex Needed by all Beginners

Trading the foreign exchange market, on the internet, can be particularly difficult for beginners who are just starting out. This is partially because of unrealistic hopes and expectations that newcomers have when entering into this world. What you should first understand, before proceeding any further with the foreign exchange market, is that this isn't a way to get rich fast. Traders who trade with Forex don't get rich in one day, week, or even within one month. You are only doing yourself a favor by accepting this early on, and preventing yourself from losing money, as well. One statistic that may surprise beginners is that almost all retail traders end up losing 90 percent of what they invest within three months. This is a loss that, for most of them, didn't have to happen.

Using a Demo Account:

One of the best tips you can take to heart, as a newcomer to the Forex world, is trading with a demo account first. Only when you can consistently win in this area, should you proceed to using real money. Every broker out there will offer a practice account to get started. Whether you are just starting out or only looking to improve your trading skills, you have to test out your strategies first to know whether they will work or not. Ideally, this is done without risking any real money, which is what a demo account offers. Then, you can move onto opening up a real account, using your new strategies with small amounts of capital. You can create your first demo account on Admiral Markets, for free, and always make sure you are acting as if your trades are 100 percent real.

The Food Chain of Retail Trading:

Being aware of the way the industry is set up is crucial, since the combination of every market participant creates your trading market. How much weight the trading party carries, in relation to the market, is kept track of and measured by the amount of money managed by that party. This includes investment banks and hedge funds worth a billion dollars, to traders that operate privately using a couple thousand dollars at a time.

The Safety of Long Term vs. Short:

In the beginning stages of foreign exchange trading, you should be focusing on and relying on preserving money, not in making it (yet). Getting rid of, or minimizing, your risks, should be your main goal and objective, at first. The easiest and quickest method for doing this is by using a trading stance that operates over the long term.

- **Investment, not Lottery:** What many beginner Forex traders don't realize is that many successful and professional traders earn their income from trends that operate over the long term, not the short. They might have orders open for multiple weeks, or even multiple years. That is what allows the foreign exchange market to operate as a way of investing, not a lottery.

- **Modesty and Patience:** What a lot of newcomer traders also don't realize is that this pursuit is often a test of character. Trading over the long term requires modesty and patience in the volume of what you trade. But the payoff is that you don't have to spend as many hours staring at your computer, which means you end up less stressed out. In addition to this, being good with numbers is always helpful when it comes to trading. Luckily, there are a few easy ways you can calculate what trading volume, leverage, and balance is needed for each instrument, in order to minimize your risks.

Simplicity is your Friend in Foreign Exchange Trading:

The absolute best system to use for Forex, when beginning with it, is one that is very simple. This means you should not overload the charts you use with an overabundance of indicators, or overload your strategy with switches or handles. When your strategy for trading is more complex, it's harder to keep track of and follow, meaning that you are less likely to succeed with it. Below is a simple example of a basic strategy for beginner trading in Forex:

- First, apply a simple, 10 day moving average. This should be applied to the chart of your choice.
- Next, each time you notice a candle closing over it, this is your signal to buy, while a handle closing below signals that you should close down the buy, opening up a sell.

This strategy is known as reversion trading, and is called such since an order getting closed will lead to opening an order in the opposite direction. Although this strategy is easy and simple, it's fallible just like any other. If you use it in a market that is trending, it may turn out to be highly profitable for you. Using it in a market that is ranging, on the other hand, could have the reverse effect that you are hoping for. In order to figure out how a strategy will perform throughout varying markets, you will have to do the necessary research and back testing to find out. Staying simple with this can be hard, especially since there are so many tools for support you can use with charts. Having a lot of tools to use doesn't matter as much as knowing how to use them properly.

Avoid Information Overload for Software:

Foreign exchange trading, for professionals and beginners alike, requires the use of software. Since there is competition between existing brokers, who all want business, the majority of trading software for foreign exchange can be used for free. As mentioned in the previous section, simplicity is usually better. There is no need to search frantically for which tools or software to use. The information in this book is more than enough to get you started. Overloading your brain with too much information will have a negative impact, so make sure you are filtering the intake of information you are exposing yourself to and being patient in your trades.

Advice on using Forex Robots:

Some beginners in Forex trading may be tempted to buy robots for trading, like Expert Advisers. Some Expert Advisers can be of assistance, but it can be difficult for these to keep earning when inevitable changes occur in the market. If you don't understand what the code that they are written in is saying, changes are you won't have success adapting the EA to function along throughout these changes. An EA could, for example, either work very well in a market that is trending, or have devastating effects such as your balance getting wiped out in mere seconds in a market that is ranging. The risk is up to you.

Learning Fundamental and Technical Analysis:

Analysis is not optional whatsoever when it comes to any kind of trading, including Forex, of course. Charts can be helpful when it comes to trading both in the long and short term. You must be taking a look at charts on a daily, monthly, and weekly basis. All guides on the subject of trading Forex, designed for beginners, will say that you need to use the following in technical analysis:

- Trending lines.
- Resistance and support lines.
- Indicators which use the above information.

On the other hand, fundamental analysis will let traders understand the way a nation's financial policies and events in the news can have an effect on its foreign exchange ecosystem.

How Trading Accounts can Differ from Each other:

Accounts for trading Forex don't only differ in the minimum deposit amount required to start. Qualities like the tight spreads, along with the minimum deposit, are among the last qualities to think about when you want to open a trading account for the long term. Instead, focus on instrument portfolios, the available leverage, and models for execution. The best platform for trading Forex is dependent on its broker, while the best broker depends on the system for trading. When it comes to Dealing Desk platform accounts, be careful unless you want to choose them based on their specific conditions.

Being Cautious in a Volatile Market:

Market volatility is what allows your activity in the trade to continue to move, but when you aren't careful with this, it can get destroyed. If a market is volatile, it will be moving sideways, allowing your orders to slip and your spreads to grow. When you are building your strategies for trading, make sure you are using volatility analysis to get a fuller picture. When you are a beginner in this market, accept the following:

- **Risk:** In the Forex market, literally anything could happen, meaning that no matter how carefully you crafted your strategy, it can be rendered useless. Crises like the one with the 2015 Swiss franc could end business for countless traders in a short amount of time.

- **Avoid News Trading:** Trading advice like the kind offered on CNN is not reliable. Do your best to avoid this if you want to succeed.

Using Trends to your Advantage:

For traders just started out, as well as the successful professionals, it's always best to make your trade decisions based on what you observer rather than what you hope or think you see. You may, for instance, believe that the U.S. currency has too high of a value and that this has been true for a long time. You then would want to short. Although you could end up being right eventually, it doesn't matter what you believe if you see a price going up. Actually, even the opinions of the most intelligent traders don't matter when a price is moving a specific way. This means that you need to trade along with those trends, not your beliefs.

Hundreds of Markets Exist:

When you start to learn about trading Forex, it can be easy to focus on the most popular currency pairs, since they offer tight spreads and plenty of volatility on a daily basis.
- **Look for Opportunities:** However, countless other opportunities exist, such as indices, energy futures, commodities, stocks, and less popular Forex pairs.
- **Diversify:** The number of markets you decide to look to for unique opportunities is your choice to make, but try not to

become limited to just one market or instrument. Limitation in the market will cause you to overtrade, so make sure that your investment is always diversified.

- **Focus on Exits too:** Keep in mind at all times that a trade stays open until it's not. The typical beginner in foreign exchange trading will focus heavily on how they will open up a trade. However, the point of exit is just as important. Without the consideration of how you'll close a deal included in your strategy, you won't have the success you want.

Think about the Legal Aspects:

Trading financially, as with Forex, is typically an activity that is legally regulated. Brokerage firm regulators that have been government assigned typically urge beginners to be careful. When you are trying to make sure conditions are secure to trade or invest, look at the following points:

- **Services:** You should look at the compensation scheme for financial services. This will define the amount of money you will be compensated in the worst-case scenario of the broker or bank losing everything by going bankrupt.

- **Segregation:** Look at the way client funds are segregated, which will assure that your money isn't being used for other purposes than trading by your broker. This will mean that your money is always there if you need to withdrawal it.

- **Procedure for Customer dealings:** Make sure that there is an efficient system for receiving customer complaints and enquiries to ensure that if an issue comes up, it can be resolved quickly, and when it can't, it's forwarded to the appropriate department. In other words, ensure that you have a protected investment.

Having a Trading Journal:

You should, at the beginning of your investment journey (and perhaps after), write all of your experiences down.

- **What to Record:** In this trading journal, you should record ideas to research further for foreign exchange trading, ideas related to trading, various ideas for how and when to close or open trades, the mistakes you've made, and your achievements. This can be used as something to reference when you are hoping to see your progress or where you could improve in your trading journey.

- **Thinking like the Owner of a Company:** You will probably find it helpful to think like the owner of a business when it comes to trading Forex. Each business owner needs a plan for their company, consistent and faithful monitoring of its developments, and auditing on a regular basis. Trying to jump too far ahead without processes or planning almost guarantees failure, and recording the events that occur along the way will help you make sure your actions don't go to waste.

- **Analyzing your Actions:** Analyzing successful trades helps you stay motivated and confident about your success, helping you push further and harder to succeed in the future. While analyzing trades that went badly can help you see where you went wrong and commit to improving and doing better next time.

The Importance of Research:

In general, when it comes to trading Forex, the more you know, the more you minimize your overall risk in losing money. No limit exists for how much information you can learn or how much money you can risk. Countless resources for information exist online, for free. Here are some ideas for resources to learn further:

- **Videos:** You can check out educational short videos about trading the foreign exchange market. These can be found on YouTube, or on some popular trading platforms.

- **Tutorials:** You can find useful information for Forex trading on tutorials and online articles about the subject, including e-books like this one.

- **Seminars:** What better way to learn than to hear what to do straight from the experts? Try listening to some Forex seminars done by professionals. There is something to be learned no matter how far you progress in your trading journey.

Most importantly, keep in mind that everything you read should be analyzed and tested for yourself to find out what works. There is no shortage of information out there, as stated before, but not all of it is quality. The only way to find out what information will serve you well is to test it out for yourself.

The Importance of the Right Attitude in Trading:

Although trading can be really fun and exciting, it also comes with plenty of stressful qualities. There are always going to be obstacles and setbacks as you learn any new skill. What you need to be aware of at all times, as a beginner, is your emotions. Strong emotions can lead you to open trades far too early and lose, or hesitate in closing and end up going out worse than you could have. Anyone involved in the trading world knows that trading psychology is an important aspect of the game. So what should you look out for?

- **Over-Confidence:** Being too confident has led many traders to end up losing by making rash decisions. Perhaps you have just experienced a huge streak of luck and feel invincible. Playing it conservatively is almost always the smarter choice.

- **Getting too Frustrated:** What causes many would-be traders to give up on the path entirely is becoming too frustrated early on. When you are studying or practicing trades on your demo account, keep track of your emotions. If you start to feel yourself getting very angry or frustrated, take a break and come back to it later. This is better than pressing on, in a moment like that.

- **Too much Hesitation:** In addition to over-confidence being a problem with trading, a lack of confidence can be just as negative. Don't let your hesitation to act on your educated strategies get in the way. Remember that action is needed in order to learn, and sometimes that involves making mistakes.

Another major factor of trading stress for newcomers is the reality that certain trades are destined to fail in the end, regardless of how well you did. Unfortunately, that's just part of the experience, and it's how the market works sometimes. Keep in mind that nothing is accomplished right away, especially not anything that is actually worthwhile and rewarding (the way trading can be). Instead, it's your overall actions and performance that will lead you to success. This is just one more great reason to stay faithful with your journal for trading.

Financing the Journey of Forex Trading:

You may have heard this before, but it's important to say. You should only be investing or trading money that you can afford to lose. Ideally, of course, this would be done without severe damage to your financial assets and future. One important principal to remember is that all successful traders have found their own unique paths to success, while all unsuccessful traders commit common mistakes. Hopefully, this chapter has given you some useful insight for how to become one of the successful ones. Use all experiences in this realm as a way to improve and get better.

Conclusion

Thank you again for buying this book!

I hope this book was able to help you to see that you can begin trading foreign exchange as soon as you have the right knowledge and information on the subject. Don't forget to keep a journal for recording all of your ideas, mistakes, and successes so that you can look back and review what you did right and wrong. This is invaluable information that you can use to get better and better at foreign exchange trading until you become one of the masters.

The next step is to follow the guidelines given to you in this book and start earning money. Again, this isn't something you will earn from immediately, but if you stick with it and make sure you practice a lot on a demo account before trying to trade your real money, there's no reason why you can't enjoy success in this arena. If countless other people have done it, why can't you?

Finally, if you enjoyed this book, then I'd like to ask you for a favor, would you be kind enough to leave a review for this book on Amazon? It'd be greatly appreciated! Click here to leave a review for this book on Amazon!

Thank you and good luck!

www.ingramcontent.com/pod-product-compliance
Lightning Source LLC
Chambersburg PA
CBHW061226180526
45170CB00003B/1177